CW0084I640

DAV
THE K
TRUE REPENTANCE

BOOK 4 (TOLD FROM 2 SAMUEL 11 – 19 AND 1 KINGS 1 – 2)

TOLD BY CARINE MACKENZIE
~ ILLUSTRATED BY GRAHAM KENNEDY ~

COPYRIGHT © 2009 CARINE MACKENZIE
ISBN 978-1-84550-489-2
PUBLISHED BY CHRISTIAN FOCUS PUBLICATIONS, GEANIES HOUSE,
FEARN, TAIN, ROSS-SHIRE, IV20 1TW, SCOTLAND, U.K.
PRINTED IN CHINA

David's men were all away from home fighting in the war. David remained at home.

Late one afternoon he got up from his couch and strolled along the roof of his house. As he looked across the courtyard he saw a beautiful woman having a bath.

"Who is she?" David asked. "I want her," he said, even after he found out she was Bathsheba, the wife of brave Uriah, one of his soldiers.

He brought her to his palace that evening.

Sometime later Bathsheba sent word to David. "I am expecting a baby."

In a panic David tried to cover up his sin. He arranged for Uriah to get some home leave. But Uriah would not go home to his wife while his comrades were fighting. David tried to get Uriah drunk but still he refused to go to his wife. David wrote a letter to Joab the captain. Uriah carried it himself. "Put Uriah in the hottest, fiercest fighting."

Uriah died in the battle just as David had planned.

Bathsheba mourned over her husband's death. David sent for her and they were married. Bathsheba gave birth to a son. But God was displeased with what David had done.

Nathan, God's prophet, was sent to speak to David. He told him a story.

There was a rich man who had lots of flocks and herds. There was a poor man who had only one little pet ewe lamb whom he loved very much.

A traveller came to visit the rich man. Instead of using one of his own flock, the rich man took the poor man's pet lamb and prepared it for dinner.

David was so angry when he heard this story. "That man deserves to die for doing such a thing."

"You are the man," said Nathan.

"God has given you much. Yet you have killed Uriah and taken his wife."

"I have sinned against the Lord," said David. He repented and asked God for forgiveness. "Wash me from my iniquity and cleanse me from my sin."

"The Lord has put away your sin," Nathan told him.

Bathsheba's baby boy became very sick. For a whole week David prayed for the baby. He would not take any food. When the baby died, the servants were afraid to tell him. David guessed when he saw them whispering.

David washed, changed his clothes, then went to the Lord's house to worship. "I cannot bring my child back. But I will go to him one day."

David and Bathsheba had another baby boy called Solomon.

David's son Absalom was very handsome. He wanted desperately to be the king of Israel. He started plotting against his father.

When anyone came to the king to settle a dispute, Absalom met him first, "If I were the judge, I would give you justice."

He became more popular than David. Even some of David's close advisors turned against him.

David was very sad and had to flee from Jerusalem, before Absalom took over the city. David knew God was still helping him and he expected God to save him.

Many fierce battles were fought between David's men and Absalom.

At the forest of Ephraim, David's army won a great victory.

Absalom was riding through the forest on his mule after the battle. He rode under a thick branch of a tree. His beautiful thick hair got caught in the branches. The mule trotted on. Absalom was left hanging by his hair.

Joab, David's general, killed Absalom.

News was brought by a messenger to King David. He heard first the good news about the victory. A second messenger arrived with other news.

When David heard that Absalom was dead, he was heartbroken.

"My son, my son Absalom," he wept. David still loved his son even although he had caused him such trouble. David returned to Jerusalem in triumph.

When David grew old, he decided that his son Solomon would be the next king. He gave him lots of good advice. "Be strong. Keep obeying all God's commandments. Be loyal to the families of those who helped me, when Absalom rebelled."

David sent Nathan the prophet to Gihon to anoint Solomon as king.

David trusted God through the good times and the bad. He faced danger, hatred and difficulties through faith in God.

He served God in his generation. After he confessed his sin, he was forgiven by his loving heavenly Father – given the gift of repentance. If we confess our sin and trust in the Lord Jesus Christ, God is faithful and just to forgive us our sin.